DIAMOND
STEPS TO
SUCCESS

REACH YOUR GOALS IN 7 STEPS

JOYCE OYEDELE

First printing: 2019

ISBN Number: 978-1-9161678-0-3

Author: Joyce Oyedele

Disclaimer and/or legal notices

The information within this book represents the author's views and opinions to date of the publication. It is designed for informational purposes only and readers are to take responsibility over successfully attaining and reaching their own goals. Every attempt has been made to provide information to equip readers in reaching their goals, but the author cannot be held responsible if goals or success is not achieved. Readers should seek professional support and advice concerning interests. The author reserves the right to alter or update the information provided within the book. Characters in this book have remained anonymous.

Connect with Joyce

Joyce Oyedele

Diamond Steps To Success

Office 25417

PO Box 6945

London. W1A 6US

Facebook: www.facebook.com/joyceoy

LinkedIn: www.linkedin.com/in/joyce-oyedele

Instagram: www.instagram.com/joyceoyedele/

Email: Joyceoyedele@gmail.com

Join the Diamond Community and receive top tips at https://bit.ly/2KhZZEW

For world-class health, skincare and weight loss products visit: www.healthwithjoy.usana.com

Dedication

To the special reader who holds this book in their hands;

seeking how they may better improve their life.

Foreword

Joyce is very passionate about personal development and adding value to people. This is very evident in how she's able to strike the necessary balance in her current commitments and being effective in gaining new grounds.

Diamond Steps To Success is a tool that will add value to people's lives. I found the summary of each chapter very useful and the reflection exercises are very practical.

In addition, the 'Success Steps' gives an opportunity to apply what you read.

Diamond Steps To Success is more than a book. It is an amazing resource with practical examples, applicable principles and inspiring stories.

Furthermore, the 'End Quotes', Appendix and Blurb makes it a value resource that anyone serious about success should have in their library.

David & Jane Adabale
Pastor and Author of *Diamond Believer*

Joyce is one of those rare, principle-centred people we've been blessed to come across in our lives. She's a lady who stands out for many reasons; not least because of her striking presence – she's also a lady who cares deeply and is hungry to learn and grow.

Diamond Steps To Success is a valuable read; especially as a summary of key stepping stones for any success journey worth taking. The timeless principles Joyce walks us through are vital, especially because each one she covers is peppered with examples from her own life-journey. This brings the information alive, allowing us to experience them in more than one dimension.

What this book doesn't tell you however, is the extent to which Joyce is a wholeheartedly caring, zealous, genuine and compassionate lady.

We trust that you're fortunate enough to meet her personally yourself one day, so that you get to witness this for yourself.

Fi Jamieson-Folland and Chris-Folland

Osteopath and Solicitor

2 Star USANA Diamond Directors

USANA Million Dollar Club Members

You are unique, very special and one who is eager to achieve even more success in your life, career or business. How do I know? It's the very reason you are now reading this book! In Diamond Steps To Success, Joyce has methodically laid out some of the barriers and challenges faced on the path to successfully achieving her goals and aspirations.

At each step, Joyce candidly shares how she felt when faced with barriers or challenges, along with the steps taken to overcome each one on the path of achieving her dreams.

The experiences Joyce shares in this book will provide the tools, ideas and confidence to face any future situation that may arise in your life.

As you will discover in Diamond Steps To Success, Joyce shares her insight on the importance of surrounding yourself with the right people to achieve your goals and ambitions.

By reading this book, you have made a sensible decision in adding Joyce to your network of trusted advisors.

Read – Learn - Implement - Achieve Your Diamond Steps To Success!

Andy O'Sullivan

Speaker and Author of:

Corporate Confidence and Communication

101 Top Secret Public Speaking Strategies

Public Speaking Success

Corporate Confidence

Pitching for Startups

Public Speaking 101

Acknowledgements

God

My foundation and rock, strong tower and friend. Thank you God for giving me the desire, confidence and wisdom to share my message in book form. Thank you for life itself and your grace. I am eternally grateful.

Family

Thank you for being a solid support and for contributing to who I am today. You have sown seeds that are slowly beginning to sprout at the appointed time. Each of you have had an impact on me and have helped me see life from different perspectives. I appreciate the love, laughter and foresight. Thank you to my parents and brother for always believing in the best for me. Special thanks to Toyin Oyedele for the hours of proof-reading, editing, support and encouragement with this book.

David and Jane Adabale

Thank you for your constant support throughout my journey. You are highly admired mentors and friends. I appreciate each moment you have encouraged, supported and blessed me with your sheer wisdom and care. God bless you and your family abundantly.

Fi Jamieson-Folland and Chris Folland

Thank you for your mentorship, love and support. The journey has not been an easy ride but with your support and guidance, I have grown to become a better person. Your energy, patience and blunt truth have always helped and for that, I am grateful. Thank you for the opportunity to sit in the presence of Dr Denis Waitley and learn from him; what a remarkable experience that was!

Andy O'Sullivan

A special thank you to Andy for the guidance and gems shared in my book journey. Your support and encouragement with the progress of my book and public speaking quest has been so helpful. I am incredibly grateful.

Friends

Thank you for your support and encouragement. You've inspired me to keep going and push on no matter what. I am grateful for your presence in my life, and I am looking forward to celebrating more of our successes together.

Abi Ogunrinde, thank you for the friendship and the book nuggets that helped encourage me on this book journey.

Michael Osei, thank you for the support and encouragement with this book process. It hasn't been easy but thank you for the insight and shared wisdom.

A particular thanks to Sandra Mighty who saw something great in me and my journey. You made me believe it was possible to pursue something I had never done before. Thank you for all the encouragement!

Thank you, Jessica Mae Obioha, for the encouragement, support and taking the time out to format this book. God bless you and the work you do.

There are so many to thank but to name a few who have made years of significant impact in my life journey: Yik Aisha Hussain, Leticia Annor, Rebecca and Damola Ademolake, Jason Agbodza, Karina Petal, Tosin Adio, Fatoumata Touray, Sinitta Lewis, Caroline Shittu, Karolina Richert, Ayo Sage, Laura Romero, Kafi Thomas, Paul Izilein, Peter Young, Sreepriya Bhowmik, Eric Buabin, Janet Ifidon, Toni Riding, Esther Ngala, Jason Hall and Joseph Unegbu, I appreciate you.

Network Marketing Friends

What a unique group! High energy, vibrant and healthy. You have encouraged me on my journey from day one and for that, I am grateful. It is always great to be part of something greater than yourself and you have given me a vehicle to bless other people's lives with. Indeed, may the vision and mission by Dr Myron Wentz to be the healthiest family on earth be accomplished. Thank you for your unending love and support.

Special thank you to Prabha Shiyani, Sara Rees, Nick Wilson, Natalie Tabony, Tom and Jess Dyer, Clarissa Escober Doonan, Nkem Ezeilo, Bash Kafi, Arzoo Arif, Bilal Iqbal, Clive Francis, Simone Teresa Lewis, Pani Dipino, Kate Keen, David Griffiths, Brian Knapp, Nick Knapp, Justin Morris, Cherry Scott, Nico Vu, Immi Ho, Christopher Duong, Joanna Bouysse, Erwin Deladerrière, Simònne Du Toit, Jennifer Eshelby, Eduardo Barreto, Matt and Megan Chionis, Paige and Daniel Hunter, Simon Chan, April London, Jen Groover, Jeremy Stansfield, David Mulham, Pasha Oliver-Carter, Brandon Hayes, Tim Cox, and many more. You have been great and shining diamond mentors in my life.

Toastmasters Friends

Thank you so much for your encouragement and support in my public speaking journey. It has and continues to be a remarkable experience meeting and hearing speeches. Thank you for always cheering me on and listening intensely, it's always a great pleasure being in your presence. Special thanks to Brian Guo, Samantha Stevens, Alice Yessouroun, Rajini Lolay, Emmanuel Odejimi, Fulvio Milesi, Florin Balan, Rob Hemsley, Alfredo Iorio, Peter Synam, Leanne Kelly, Chris Pass, Wayne Reid and many more.

Church Friends

Thank you to all I have served with and your great impact. Special thanks to the founder, Dr Tayo Adeyemi for your relentless pursuit for the attendees and congregation to discover, develop and deploy their God given gifts. Hearing your teaching ignited something great within me and I have been inspired ever since.

Pastor Michael Olawore, you were a man of excellence and relentless love for God's people. Thank you for all the prayers, dedication and love. Indeed "Everything is made beautiful in its time".

Pastor Kola Taiwo, thank you for your dedication to the Church and self-sacrifice. Goodness and mercy continue to follow you and your family all the days of your life.

Students

There is a great love I have for each of you. You are FULL of so much potential! Get the education you need and apply yourselves. I believe in you greatly and am grateful for the opportunity to impact your life in a positive way. Go and change the world!

◆ Introduction ◆

About the author

My name is Joyce Oyedele. My sole purpose of writing this book is to help you reach your goals successfully based on some of the experiences I've had in reaching my own goals. Working in the field of business, education, health and ministry has given me insight and experiences that I believe are valuable to share with you.

I have a BSc in Psychology from the University of Surrey and a Diploma in Counselling Psychology from City, University of London. Understanding how the mind functions is an incredible art which has continued to intrigue me. I enjoy growing and learning about how this helps a person to become even more successful in life.

I chose the book title 'Diamond Steps To Success' because I believe that some of the goals and successes we aspire to reach require us to go through a process similar to that of a diamond.

A diamond is a precious stone that is required to go through rigorous processes to become valuable; beautifully cupped in the grasp of a piece of jewellery. As individuals striving towards our goals, we too need to go through such process to shine in any situation we find ourselves in. I am inspired by the diamond; such a precious beautiful shining stone that comes in all shapes and sizes, refracting light at all angles. Our goals can be like this once we commit to the process.

I am extremely passionate about helping people fulfil their potential to become the best version of themselves. Sharing my message through this book and public speaking opportunities excites me a great deal. My desire is that as you read this, something will shift in you for the better, which will in turn inspire you to take the necessary steps to reach your goals successfully.

You may wonder what qualified or propelled me to write a book on success, since there are many other books of this category out there! However, this book entails some of my learnings and journeys that have helped me overcome obstacles and reach my goals. As a British African, I didn't find many books from UK authors which represented my background or related to what I had experienced in London. Therefore, I decided that it was a good chance to share my message to inspire others in reaching their goals and visions.

You'll find at the end of each chapter 'Reflections' and a 'Success Step' where you can jot down some thoughts that will help you on your diamond steps to success journey. The questions and exercises are designed to stimulate your mind and being in order to help you process the next steps to achieving your goals.

My hope is that you implement these steps to help you get closer to achieving your Diamond Goals!

Contents

Contents

◆ Chapter 1 ◆

◆ Chapter 1 ◆

The Beginning:

Seeing the End from the Beginning

It's often quite difficult to find where we should start when we think of setting our goals. It's assumed that people 'know' what goals they should be setting, but sometimes it is just confusing! Therefore, the first step is to think about what you want the end result of a particular project to be. In the process of making a diamond ready to become jewellery, it is important for the miners to know what it is they are looking for. If they do not give enough thought to what they would like to see in the end, they would not know how to plan or use their time effectively. Once miners know what it is they want to achieve, they can begin the process!

Identifying Your Diamond Goal

So, what are you looking to find? When identifying your 'Diamond Goal', you will find that this goal requires you to stretch and grow; it is a goal that is BIG and isn't easily achievable. It is not something you achieve by mistake but a goal that will take intentional effort and focus. It is something that will take time and careful planning to achieve. Most commonly, a goal like this will be something that will inevitably make you a better person by building your character, your mind and your position. Your Diamond Goal will help you grow as a person, positively impact the lives of others and position you for greater opportunities. You would want this goal to be something that is specific, measurable, achievable, realistic and timely.

In the diamond making process, the manager of the miners knows what type of diamonds they are looking to retrieve. They will consider the colour of the diamond, outline how many diamonds they want to retrieve and set out a specific time-frame when they would want to have the diamonds. This can involve quite a number of people and careful planning. The manager will most probably have a visual representation of what it is the miners are looking for and direct them accordingly.

When working towards finding your Diamond Goal, it helps to visualise what you want to see at the end of a project or situation. Seeing the end from the beginning will help you locate and refine your goal. A vision of what you desire helps you paint a clearer picture of what you  want in life and it also helps you identify the steps that would help you get there. If your vision is clear, it will help pull you through the tough roadblocks that will attempt to stand in your way.

Visualising Your Diamond Goal

When you think about your goal, use your five senses to think about how it will feel once it is achieved. Achieving a Diamond Goal should make you feel excited, exuberant and elevated. Generally, you would have higher energy levels which would give you the gusto to press on. Using your mind to paint a picture of what you want to see will help you refine your goal.

Sight: What does your goal look like when you visualise it? What can you imagine seeing when your goal has been reached? What do you want to see? Who will be around you when you've reached your goal? This is a powerful practice to do, especially as it imprints on your subconscious mind and adds a bit of realism to your goal.

Touch: Is your goal so strongly visualised in your mind that you can almost touch it? What are you wearing and how does it feel? Are you holding anything? What does it feel like? The stronger the feeling of reaching your goal, the more likely it will materialise into something physical. It could also help having some physical imagery or objects around you which represents what achieving your goal means to you.

Smell: Now, this one may seem a little strange. How does one actually smell their goal? Well, let me ask you this, have you ever watched something on TV, let's take for instance, a person baking cake and you thought "Mmmm… I can imagine what that must smell like!" Well it's the same premise here; imagine what your goal smells like. How does that smell make you feel? At this point, the aim is to immerse yourself into your goal via your senses, so engage this sensory aspect as well.

Taste: You may have often heard of the phrase 'the taste of success' or 'I was so close I could almost taste it', this doesn't refer to the physical taste of something. It refers to the feeling tasting something amazing gives us. Imagine for a moment that you just took a bite of your favourite dish; how does that make you feel? Happy? Radiant? Keep that feeling because that positive feeling will be similar to what it will feel like when you reach your goal.

Hear: Last but not least, think about what you will hear when you reach your goal. Will people be around you congratulating you for completing your goal? Will you hear loved ones express their joy when you have achieved what you have set out to do? Visualising what you will say and hear from others also helps to make your goal more tangible and realistic. These factors count towards finding and forming what you desire to be your Diamond Goal.

Your Why

Seeing the end from the beginning helps you in your decision making, and subsequently, it propels your steps to move forward. There are countless numbers of obstacles, setbacks and challenges on the way to achieving your Diamond Goal. These may include practical challenges, disappointments and unexpected difficulties. When barriers present themselves, it is important to remember why you had your goal in the first place. Perhaps it's something you wanted to achieve because you knew it would help others, or give you a sense of satisfaction. Whichever it is, remind yourself!

Visualising what you desire in your goal and remembering *why* you started it will help you take the steps you need to get there. Sometimes we find that the difficulty is incredibly intense! It is in times like this that it becomes important to fan the fire on the reason why you started in the first place. Reminding yourself of the result, especially if it has to do with others, will give you enough fuel to keep going and press on! A key to keeping the visualisation active for your Diamond Goal is to set constant reminders. Write it on your phone, on a notepad and even on your wall. Keep a constant reminder of what it is you want to achieve. By doing so, you will work towards its fulfilment.

You may have a Diamond Goal to write your own book to inspire the next generation and leave a legacy. This is not an easy goal to achieve! However, constantly seeing yourself in your mind as a successful writer

A key to keeping the visualisation active for your Diamond Goal is to set yourself constant reminders.

of a book and writing your goal down plainly will help you step towards that goal. When you constantly use all your senses to engage your mind, you will start to pick up on cues that will help you achieve that goal. The action that follows will involve conjuring up an idea and dedicating time to start your writing process. As you keep this image within your mind, you will take bold steps towards publishing your own book. You'll come up with a book title, an idea of the length and the time you want to complete it. As you constantly visualise this goal and work towards it, you will come across roadblocks such as losing motivation in your journey or struggling to find the right publishers. These obstacles will try to derail you, however, if you remind yourself of *why* you started in the first place and visualise what you desire to achieve in the end, you will persevere and become a successful writer of your own book.

Your Subconscious

If you are serious about your Diamond Goal, take time out of your day to visualise the type of goal you want to achieve. We know this will not be an easy task (knowing how busy life can be). However, if you

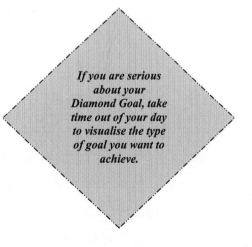

If you are serious about your Diamond Goal, take time out of your day to visualise the type of goal you want to achieve.

intentionally take time out to visualise, you will be that much closer to reaching your goal. This will help you create a bigger picture of what you desire in your end result. Doing this consistently will help your subconscious mind influence your conscious mind to make your goal a reality. This is because the subconscious mind is very powerful and cannot tell the difference between an extremely powerful visualisation and realityi.

There is a link between the subconscious mind and the physical realm. For example, have you ever experienced a time when you were almost fast asleep and in your dream, you tripped over something or fell off a building? Has the shock from that been so intense that it woke you up? This happens because your body has reacted to the visual image in your subconscious mind. If you become more and more intentional about this, your body and subconscious mind will work together to help you fulfil the goal of what you have been constantly visualising. It may come in an unexpected way or slightly different to what you had imagined, but it all boils down to using your mind to create your reality. There is also a link between your visualisation and emotion. You can use your emotion to stimulate your mind into helping you get closer to your goal. The more you visualise and add emotion to your visualisation, the more you work on the same energy level as your vision. As this occurs, you 'trick' your subconscious mind into believing that it

The more you visualise and add emotion to your visualisation, the more you work on the same energy level as your vision.

is real. This is why it is incredibly important to surround yourself with inspirational images of what you want to achieve and what you desire. Your subconscious mind is sensitive; working like a sponge – particularly with creating images. What you see constantly shapes how you see things and what you believe is possible[ii].

For example, a person may think that going on an all-inclusive holiday to the Bahamas is an impossible dream. However, if they are able to find images and create a vision board, they are more likely to turn that vision into reality. This happened to me when I put up pictures of Italy in my surroundings. I imagined what it would be like to visit the country. A few years later, I found myself travelling to Rome and Venice! It may take time to manifest, and you will need to be intentional about taking the physical steps necessary, but doing this helps you get closer to your goal.

I remember when I had a goal of achieving the leadership title of 'Silver Director' within the network marketing company I work with. A network marketing company is a company that distributes products and services to and through people and their networks. To achieve the leadership title, I envisioned being a Silver Director in my mind and formulated a step by step plan of how I would achieve it. That goal was extremely challenging, but I practised constant visualisation, self-belief and actions. There were times I didn't think it was possible because of the doubt, misunderstandings and rejection I experienced from others and myself. In fact, those setbacks brought my energy levels so low that I started to internalise and believe negative thoughts. I wasn't aware of the challenges that would come along with my goal, and I sometimes experienced the doubt of whether I could handle the pressure or not. However, instead of dwelling on the challenges, I reminded myself of the reason I joined the company in the first place and thought about the lives that I could help if I reached my Diamond Goal of Silver Director. I imprinted the image on my mind and disciplined myself to work tirelessly. This involved placing the goal in various visible places, talking about it constantly *and* taking action without undermining my abilities. That experience was the physical part of the steps I took to reach my goal, but there was a spiritual aspect too. I believe God shifted things to work in my favour and I was graced with the push and grit needed to press forward! I prayed, asked and He answered. Consequently, I became the first female British African in Europe to become a Silver Director at the age of 26.

In conclusion, like the manager in the mining company, you will need to see the end at the beginning to achieve your Diamond Goal. When you mix this with your senses, faith and action, you will accomplish great things! As your subconscious mind is visually more sensitive to images, surrounding yourself with what you desire in picture form will help you get closer to your goals. Doing this will also help you see it in your mind more clearly and keep you on track. Keep going and don't lose sight of your Diamond Goal!

"Keep the image of the end from the beginning and you will inevitably take the necessary steps to make it your reality!"

Joyce Oyedele

Key Points:

- A Diamond Goal is something you want to achieve that will inevitably make you a better person by building your character, your mind and your position.

- Your visualisation and senses can be used as a tool to influence your subconscious mind to reach your Diamond Goal.

- Ask God for help and strength when working towards your goals.

Reflections

What do you see as your Diamond Goal?

_____

_____

_____

What does the accomplishment of it look like?

_____

Feel like?

_____

Smell like?

_____

Taste like?

_____

Sound like?

_____

_____

When is the best time for you to practice your visualisation?

_____

_____

What images are you going to intentionally surround yourself with?

_____

_____

Where are you going to put these images (e.g. Phone screensaver, room wall, mirror, bathroom)?

Success Step 1

Find pictures representing the goals you have and put it somewhere you will see every day.

◆ Chapter 2 ◆

◆ Chapter 2 ◆

Mining Diamonds:

Identifying What Your Diamond Goal is Worth

Whenever we set goals, we need to identify its worth and the sacrifices it will take to get achieve them. During the pipe mining process, the earth around the diamond is crushed and flushed with water. Miners need to determine whether the process of obtaining the pipes, digging into the depths of the earth and extracting the coals is worth the effort that is required to get the diamond out. This process takes so much effort, money and time. They may be working on the extraction process for days, months or even years. However, because they know that the end result of the coal process will result in a highly priced diamond with so much value attached to it, they persevere and proceed.

Knowing the Cost

The diamond process is similar to working towards our Diamond Goals. We need to weigh the costs, and decide whether or not we want to go ahead. Sometimes we don't have the knowledge of all it would involve, but if we believe and strongly desire the end result – we will have faith and go ahead.

What is your Diamond Goal worth to you? That Diamond Goal will definitely be more challenging than something you have accomplished in the past. However, as you constantly remind yourself of why you are going for it, you will renew the energy that it takes to go forward. When you have settled in your mind that this is what you want, you need to take time out to think about what it will cost. You'll know that if you want something different, it will require a change in action to get there. The phrase 'You'll always get what you've always gotten if you keep doing what you've always done!' has a lot of truth to it. In order to get results different from what you have now, you'll need to do something different. With this action, there will be a cost. It's important to think about whether it is worth it or not.

You'll always get what you've always gotten if you keep doing what you've always done!

Being Aware of Others

Sometimes people go for the attainment of their goal no matter the cost involved. Their pursuit may even cause harm to others in the process. For example, I knew of a woman who wanted to become a Senior Manager in a company. This was her goal but she went about it in the most conniving manner. She drew close to the senior members of the company and spoke negatively about her fellow colleagues in order to make herself look better. As she did this, she would boast about her personal achievements and why she thinks she was the best candidate for the job. The team under her management felt undervalued and disrespected, but continued to work as this was their job. As she spoke negatively about her colleagues, she ruined their reputation. Her mind-set was that she would rise by putting others down. Though initially, it seemed to work in her favour and she did indeed get a higher position – she lost the trust of the Director and her colleagues. Her behaviour showed that she was not a good team-player, and lacked the ability to lead others in an effective way. Eventually, she was sacked for maltreatment of employees and had to find another job elsewhere. Yikes! If your pursuit towards your Diamond Goal ruins and knocks others back along the way, think again! It is advisable to check in with your morals and be conscious when striving towards your goals.

Your Identity and Values

Is your Diamond Goal something that conflicts with your identity and values? We often don't achieve the goals that conflict with who we see ourselves as. If we don't identify with the goal, then it would be even more difficult for us to achieve it. An ambitious woman who does not see herself as a housewife is very unlikely to become a woman who stays at home *solely* to raise the family. It really does depend on how you see yourself, as this will determine what you are willing to sacrifice.

Challenges

You can decide whether your Diamond Goal is worth the challenges you will face. These challenges come for several reasons. Challenges question the strength of your conviction concerning the goal you have set. Each time it shows up, it forces you to consider whether you are serious about your goal or not. So, really, a challenge is a question. Each time it appears, it is asking you – how badly do you want this? What is it worth to you?

Unfortunately, the challenges do not tell you how long they will be around. It could be for an hour, a day, a month or sometimes even years! It's easy to feel burnt out, extremely low or completely demotivated. Take a break, feed yourself with positive life-

Challenges question the strength of your conviction concerning the goal you have set.

filled affirmations, and remind yourself of why you started in the first place. Once you have given yourself time, restart when you feel refreshed and feed your mind with faith as you give your goal another push. You will find that you have become even stronger than when you started.

When you embark on journeys that involve persistence, discipline and the right attitude, you will face many barriers. These barriers may come in the form of people, situations and definite inconveniences! Remember, this is all part of your diamond process.

The people you love, care for and cherish may try to stop you. Their words and actions may be unintentional, but what is important is that you know with conviction where you want to go. They may remind you of your past failures or habits. Stand strong! Perhaps, they are trying to keep you safe within their comfort zone. However, because you have seen the end from the beginning and you know what your Diamond Goal is worth, you can choose to press on to achieve that end.

Dealing with Critics

Criticisms can be quite difficult to handle when the people who express them are family or close friends. You may strongly desire that they cheer you on and give you the greatest approval and support, however, unfortunately, this may rarely happen – especially in the first instance.

The shock of the change and process you are going through makes them uncomfortable and so as a response, they may attempt to stop you from attaining your goal. They may not realise how their perceived lack of support is affecting you and your trust in them. At this point, you have the choice to distance yourself from them and restrict your communication or remain in their presence. If you believe their opinions more than your convictions, you run the risk of not growing and remaining in your comfort zone. This will most certainly not help you achieve your goals.

If you believe their opinions more than your convictions, you run the risk of not growing and remaining in your comfort zone.

Be sure to identify whether the opinions of others are for your best interest or theirs. The other side of the coin is that your family and close friends could *actually* be trying to genuinely help you, but you do not perceive it that way. It's worth asking them the reason for the criticism and observing how you could learn from it. There are some people who appreciate hearing outside voices of guidance so as to help them reach their goal, and people who solely rely on their own inner voice (I personally like a mixture of both). It may not be easy to spot who is trying to help you and who is not, or whether their words of advice are for your own good or theirs, but be open to hearing what they have to say. If it gets despairingly negative and you find your energy levels continuingly diminishing, then it may be best to keep a distance until you're able to evaluate your situation and what is right for you.

I remember a time when I was working so hard to generate sales of a product in a company, I would invest a great amount of time and money visiting people, travelling and running events. The desire and pursuit of my goal was a magnificent obsession that needed that dedicated time and energy. However, whilst I was in this vortex of momentum, others around me did not quite understand what the fuss was all about. From my perception, they were critical about the sacrifice of effort, time and money. They claimed that I should stop and that I had been misled. I had to decipher whether they were genuinely trying to help me or whether they were being a hindrance. However, I discovered that the more I listened to them, the less motivated I became. I decided to remain focused on my goal and revisit the reason behind it. This kept me going and as a result, people enjoyed the benefits of the product on their health and I reached my goal.

Another cost you need to consider is the discredit and criticism you may get from people who genuinely do not want you to succeed in life. Some may call them 'Haters'… 'Enemies of progress'… 'The devil!' These people really do not like to see others progress because they feel that your progression takes away their own opportunity to progress. They are unaware and do not believe that success and prosperity are abundant. Success and prosperity *are* abundant and it is my belief that God is the source of it. Rather than focusing on the critics, focus on the one who gave you the desire and passion to go for your goal. You may not realise how much reaching your goal is going to help

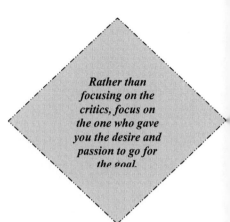

Rather than focusing on the critics, focus on the one who gave you the desire and passion to go for the goal.

others in the long run. It may be the very thing that encourages them to reach *their* own goal! The journey is challenging, but never be afraid to ask for help. If you ask for help, the unseen realm has a way of manifesting help into the physical realm. Help will come for your journey in the most unexpected ways.

This takes faith and a humble heart in order to ask, believe and receiveiii. As much as possible, do not pay attention to those who do not desire your wellbeing. When you pay too much attention to them, you are saying that their opinion is worth more than your Diamond Goal. Don't focus on the critics; instead, focus on the One who gives you help where and when you need it.

Belief

So, we've looked at dealing with criticism, but having faith and belief can also be challenging! You can start to question yourself again. However, feeding your belief through reading and watching life-giving messages will give you a boost. In my experience, scriptures from spiritual books helped me to align with my goals as it reminded me of *why* God laid it in my heart to achieve. Remember, everything that has been accomplished in our lives has taken some element of belief to bring it into manifestation. It may not happen exactly as you want it to, or

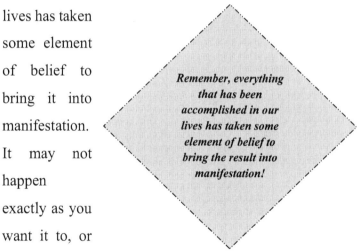

Remember, everything that has been accomplished in our lives has taken some element of belief to bring the result into manifestation!

even *when* you want it to, but it has a way of working out.

For those who do believe in God, they have the special gift of prayer. Prayer is a free gift which allows you to connect to the eternal source[iv]. There are just some things that cannot be accomplished on your own. Therefore, if you are a believer, use the gift that has been given to you and pray for the manifestation of what you desire – your Diamond Goal. If it is right and destined for you, you will surely receive it in due time. If not, trust that something better will come your way.

Disruptions

Is your Diamond Goal still worth it when things don't happen exactly the way you want them to? As you work on your goal, you may find circumstantial challenges occurring daily! Have you ever experienced days when things haven't gone your way from the moment you woke up? One thing after another – your alarm didn't go off, you woke up late, you rushed to get ready, there was no hot water, your keys weren't where you left them and the transport was running late! Yes, we have all had days like that, and we want the day to be over as soon as it starts! However, again, these situations are asking you – what is your Diamond Goal worth? These sorts of challenges tend to happen when you are extremely close to your goal.

However, a quote that always encourages me when things like that happen comes from Les Brown in which he says "When things go wrong, don't go with them!"ᵥ The good news is that you have been equipped with the power to

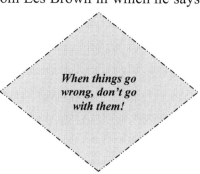

When things go wrong, don't go with them!

overcome and persevere. Choose to not go down with your challenges, and decide in your mind that your Diamond Goal is worth it!

I remember when I was studying for my Counselling Psychology Diploma, there were modules that were extremely intense, which required self-reflection and detailed analysis of theories and research. There was a time when so many daily challenges showed up and I was beginning to lose motivation. However, revisiting why I was drawn to the course and being committed to my own personal development, I decided to press on. It was after that time of feeling the temptation to give up; I broke through and attained my Diamond Goal of being awarded with the Graduate Certificate in Counselling Psychology.

What's the Benefit?

Working towards something of worth takes sacrifice, self-discipline and personal development. Be dedicated to what you are working towards and decide whether you deem the Diamond Goal and your vision worth it. Do an internal cost/benefit analysis or write it in a journal, notepad or even on a piece of paper as a reminder. Ask yourself questions like, how does this goal benefit me? How will it benefit others? Are there social, emotional, physical, financial or psychological benefits? If so, what are they? After weighing up the benefits, start listing the costs and weigh them against the benefits to get a clearer picture of what is involved in order to achieve your goal.

I remember when I had the goal of going to as many personal development classes for one year, I took extra classes on building my skills and sacrificed time to attend. It was difficult as I had to forgo other projects and commitments. However, I thought that the more I develop myself, the more value I have to offer to others and the more growth I experience. At the end of the year, I reached my goal and was awarded the 2009 Outstanding Commitment to Personal Development SUGAR Award. My encouragement to you is to take a look at what your goal is going to cost you and keep going until it is achieved.

As you work towards your Diamond Goals and successes, you inevitably inspire others to do the same (especially if your efforts are displayed publically). As I worked on my goals in Network Marketing, I helped others and shared (and continue to share) experiences on my journey towards my goal to encourage them to reach their various goals. This was mainly through social media and face to face interaction. As a result, in 2017, I was recognised for the European Teamwork Award in front of thousands at the company's international convention celebration. It took consistent effort, sacrifice and growth, but it was worth it! My encouragement to you is to commit to your diamond journey and inspire others in pursuit of your goal.

In conclusion, when planning to work on your Diamond Goal, it is crucial to think about the worth of your goal and what the cost of achieving it will be. Your goal may be something that improves the lives of others, but it will come at a cost you. Ensure that you are setting a goal that aligns with your values and identity, as if it doesn't, it would be nearly impossible to reach. Fuel your faith and belief by using life-filled words to help you deal with critics and challenges that present themselves. Finally, think about the benefits of reaching your goal and keep this in your vision to help you achieve the successful completion of what you visualised.

"Nothing in the world is worth having or worth doing unless it means effort, pain, difficulty… I have never in my life envied a human being who led an easy life. I have envied a great many people who led difficult lives and led them well."

Theodore Roosevelt vi

Key Points:

- Consider the cost and sacrifice you will need to make to achieve your Diamond Goal.

- Challenges will refine your character by testing your faith and conviction.

- Consider whether the people around you have a positive or negative influence on you.

Reflections

What is your Diamond Goal worth?

What is the sacrifice you need to make?

What are the range of benefits you could experience in reaching your Diamond Goal?

How can you feed your faith and belief in reaching your goals?

How will you respond to critics?

When your day isn't going as you would want it to, what will you do?

_____

_____

_____

Success Step 2

Determine the sacrifices you are willing to make to achieve your Diamond Goal.

Chapter 3

◆ Chapter 3 ◆

Ore Extraction:

Removing Limiting Beliefs and Fear

When we have a Diamond Goal, we can often feel like we are not good enough. When we look at our goal, we question whether we are smart enough, qualified enough or experienced enough to reach it. This is because of the fear we feel, and the limiting beliefs that we think. We need to go through the process of removing the negative thoughts that block us from achieving our goals. This can be likened to removing the diamond ore from the depths of the earth and discovering the true diamond embedded inside. During the actual diamond process, the diamond ore is extracted from the earth and is deposited on the seabed. In the journey towards your goal, it is like the ore that surrounds the diamond is the limitations and the goal is the diamond within. Therefore, it is crucial that you remove them in order to achieve your Diamond Goal.

When working towards our Diamond Goal, fear can enter our minds and stop us from taking the right actions. This can leave us in a state of inertia. Newton's First Law of Motion states "…an object at rest tends to stay at rest and an object in motion tends to stay in motion."vii If we don't take action, we are not going to reach our goal. It may not be that we don't *want* to take action but because we let the fearful thoughts paralyse us. When this happens, we tend to procrastinate

We need to go through the process of removing the negative thoughts that block us from achieving our goals.

and push the deadline further. Sometimes, we give ourselves the *illusion* that we are getting things done by ticking off irrelevant things on our to-do lists, but it's important to focus on the tasks that will actively help us reach our Diamond Goal.

I have had first-hand experience of this, especially with writing this book! When I decided to write the book, I knew that I wanted to use it to encourage people who were finding reaching their goals difficult. However, I was constantly distracted by all the other irrelevant tasks and other 'to do's'. I would also have negative thoughts such as 'I can't do this'… 'I have never written a book, so why should I try?'… 'What will critics say?' However, to overcome the inertia, I substituted all the negative thoughts and fears with positive thoughts, and focussed more on the positive impact it could make and how I would feel on its completion. This gave me the motivation to move forward by dedicating time and effort to its completion. It was a constant battle but as a result, you are now holding the outcome of my dedication in your hand today!

We sometimes fear that we will fail, and that we will embarrass ourselves by trying to reach our Diamond Goal. We have been programmed to avoid mistakes like the plague, and follow the path set before us by others. I know this feeling and I can relate to it. Growing up in the UK and being fully engrossed in the old education system, I learnt that he who makes the fewest mistakes wins and lives the happiest life. But what I came to realise is that without mistakes, my character will miss the key ingredients for growth and learning that only present themselves through mistakes.

Coming from an African background meant that education was extremely important, and with that came a hefty weight of protection. Though all the guarding and protection was well-intentioned, it did rob me off of some practical life experiences. I decided to take the opportunity to move out and find my own feet when I went to university. I made mistakes, but learnt how to adapt to all sorts of people. The fear of failure was managed and allowed me to experience more than I would have without them. Therefore, I encourage you with the well-known author Susan Jeffers by saying 'Feel the fear and do it anyway!'viii

Sometimes, it is the limiting beliefs that we are unaware of that block us from achieving our goals. Until we remove it, we will be stuck. Take this

Feel the fear and do it anyway!

analogy as an example; imagine getting into your car one morning and turning on the engine. You look in your rear-view mirror, side mirrors and windshield window, and all seem clear! You move your gear stick to drive mode, indicate, push down your handbrake and step on the accelerator pedal, but your car doesn't move! You find it strange and so you step on the pedal even more only to hear your engine revving but still, no movement! You wonder what is going on and so you stop the engine, pull your hand break up and as look out through your window, you see a passer-by pointing to the floor in front of your car. So, you get out of your car, look to where the passer-by pointed, only to see a hefty rock wedged between your tyre and the pavement. You use your foot to remove the rock, get back into the car and start the engine. Finally, your car starts to move forward and you are on your way!

That, my friends, is exactly like limiting beliefs. They are hard to spot and just like the rock in the analogy, you may not even be aware that they are there! The limiting beliefs may have been planted in your subconscious mind when you were younger. The beliefs stemming from this place of cognition and experience may form limiting beliefs that are blocking you from reaching your desired destination – your Diamond Goal. Sometimes, it may take someone else to help you realise that it is even there. Until you remove it, you will find that you are not smoothly moving in the direction that you truly desire.

Let me give a small personal anecdote. One evening, I decided to do some cleaning and was shredding paper. Each time I put the paper through the shredder, it kept getting stuck. This happened over and over again, and I had no idea why it kept happening. I looked, but didn't see what was causing the paper to jam. I tried to put fewer papers in at a time, then added more, folded the paper and tried all sorts of combinations… still to no avail. I finally got fed up, unplugged the machine and peeped through. Right in the middle and buried deep down (and I mean deep) was a wedge of crumpled paper, it was so small and seemingly insignificant. I tried to dig it out by turning the machine upside down, sideways and even used sharp equipment (which I don't recommend!). Finally, after all attempts, the wedged paper fell out! The crumpled paper was an obstacle and once I had removed it, the paper that needed shredding flowed through freely and I was able to carry on with my shredding. This is like the limiting beliefs we have in our mind. We cannot see them, but they may be the barrier that blocks the great flow of positive things flowing our way. We live our lives and go along without realising that these limiting beliefs are blocking our progress and success. However, when we become conscious of them, we can take the necessary steps to remove them.

But how do we know what these limiting beliefs are? I'm glad you asked! Well, you'll be able to find out what your limiting beliefs are by taking notice of the thoughts or situations that constantly crop up in your life to form stumbling blocks. For example, when I was working towards a leadership position, a thought kept reoccurring in my mind: 'You can't do this; there are no other black females

You'll be able to find out what your limiting beliefs are by taking notice of the thoughts or situations that constantly crop up in your life to form stumbling blocks.

who have reached this goal!' This thought was blocking me from believing in myself and taking the active steps required to go forward. I identified it as it continued to show up in my thought and speech. People would notice me giving my skin colour as an excuse for not achieving the goal. However, I went through coaching sessions and used several techniques for its removal.

These are some I have used:

Prayer and Meditationix

This is sometimes overlooked or even seen as a 'last resolve.' However, meditating and praying with scriptures that speak the truth will help you overcome the limiting belief. Sometimes, this takes more time and patience than what you are

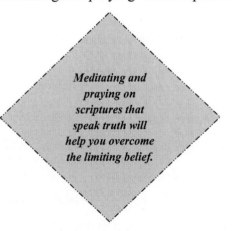

Meditating and praying on scriptures that speak truth will help you overcome the limiting belief.

willing to give, but will bring results if done consistently. For example, I would meditate on the scripture 'The joy of the Lord is my strength' when the limiting thought of 'I'm too weak' came to mind. Prayer can also be very helpful in helping you to become more conscious about what may be blocking your success in reaching your goal. You can also pray for divine intervention and connection with others who are connected to your Diamond Goal, purpose and destiny.

Floating Balloon$_x$

The balloon technique is a visual technique used to remove limiting beliefs. Find a place where you can take some time to be quiet. See in your mind one limiting belief that reoccurs and rate how strongly you feel it is true e.g. 10 being extremely strong. Imagine blowing the negative thought into a balloon, tying it up and letting it free into the distance. Vividly imagine it floating away into the blue sky, so far until it cannot be seen anymore, and then rate how strongly you feel towards the negative belief. Do this repeatedly until the rated number falls below 3. This is a visual way of using your mind that could help get rid of some of the limiting beliefs you may have about yourself.

Distant Sea

Similar to the balloon, you can use water as a visual technique to remove your limiting beliefs. Imagine you are on a calm serene beach where you can see the never-ending sea. You then hear the limiting thought and write it on a piece of paper. You roll it up and place it into a bottle. Now, imagine the bottle floating off into the distance until it no longer can be seen. You can then replace the thought with a more powerful and positive confession. This done repeatedly can help you to reach a point where you no longer identify with the limiting belief and are able to move forward without it getting in your way. This is a technique I used when I wanted to replace the limiting belief that said 'I am not qualified to do this job.' with 'I am capable of learning the skills require to do this job!'

Remember, once the limiting belief has been removed, it is important to replace it with a more liberating and wholesome thought. In my case, referring back to the example I mentioned earlier, instead of saying to myself

'You can't do this; there are no other black females that have reached this Diamond Goal!' I replaced it with the thought 'You CAN do this, you will be the FIRST black female to reach this Diamond

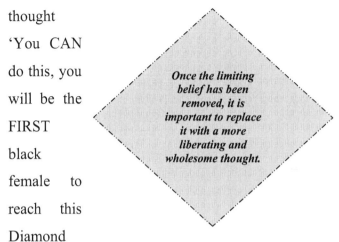

Once the limiting belief has been removed, it is important to replace it with a more liberating and wholesome thought.

Goal!' By repeatedly making this affirmation, I was able to reach my goal by removing the limiting beliefs and fear.

When you are faced with an opportunity to reach your Diamond Goal, self-doubt and questions will start to flood in and cloud your thought processes. The doubt of others can also add additional weight to how you see yourself and your decision making. What we might not realise we are doing at this stage is creating our own barriers and stopping ourselves from stepping into our own opportunity. The quote "…"What if I fall?" Oh but my darling, What if you fly?" xi By Erin Hanson comes to mind. Instead of asking what if this goes wrong? Ask yourself what if this goes well? Instead of asking what if I don't achieve it? Instead ask yourself, what if I do? Instead of thinking I'm not good enough; think I am MORE than enough and so on. When you do this, it helps create a positive mind-set and helps you to move forward.

You continue to remove limiting beliefs by developing yourself and enhancing who you are. To develop yourself, consider reading books so as to help you become more confident and assured. There are hundreds of books on growing yourself and removing self-limiting beliefs. Take time out to read through as they will share some insights on how you can move

You continue to remove limiting beliefs by developing yourself and enhancing who you are.

forward towards becoming the person you need to be to achieve your Diamond Goals. There are also personal development seminars, meet-ups and groups that will sharpen your skills and self-belief. Keep yourself motivated by investing in these – they'll help you reach your goals.

In conclusion, fear and limiting beliefs attempt to stop us from achieving our goals. However, through using techniques of prayer, meditation and visualisation, you can work on removing those limiting beliefs. It will take time but with consistency, your mind-set will change towards your ability to reach your goals. Like the diamond process, we need to extract the diamond ore and remove the limitations from our mind-set. My encouragement to you is to keep going and make your positive confessions as each of these will help you grow in belief, and reach your Diamond Goal.

"You are far too smart to be the only thing standing in your way."

Emma Kate [xii]

Key Points:

- Become aware of the continuous limiting thoughts that come to your mind when working towards your Diamond Goal.

- Work on removing the limiting beliefs and fear that you experience so as to move forward towards your goal.

- Replace your limiting beliefs with more empowering truth-filled affirmations.

Reflections

What thoughts regularly come to your mind when you set a goal?

_____

_____

_____

What type of fears do you experience when working towards your Diamond Goal?

_____

_____

_____

What limiting beliefs regularly occur for you?

_____

_____

_____

What techniques will you use to remove these limiting beliefs?

_____

_____

_____

What words are you going to replace these beliefs with?

_____

_____

_____

How will you continue to develop yourself?

_____

_____

_____

Success Step 3

Repeatedly affirm the opposite of a reoccurring self-limiting belief that you may have about yourself.

◆ Chapter 4 ◆

◆ Chapter 4 ◆

Rough Diamond:

Using your Thoughts, Emotions, Words and Actions

In the journey towards overcoming barriers and reaching our goals, we may find that situations are working against us. However, we may be unaware that it is our thoughts that are perpetuating the situation further. When the diamond ore is extracted, the diamonds within are in their rough state. It is crucial for the rough diamonds to be refined through mills and grinders in order to bring out the true value and beauty of the diamond stone. The rough state symbolises our state of being before we reach our Diamond Goals. We need to use our thoughts, feelings, words and actions to reach our goals.

For you to reach your Diamond Goal, you will need to make full use of your thoughts to attract what you need. You may find it strange that I use the word 'attract' however, there is a law of attraction that can work in your favour when striving to reach your goals. The law of attraction is

We need to use our thoughts, feelings, words and actions to reach our goals.

based on the law of vibration. Everything, including your very being, vibrates. You continuously attract the energy that you send out every day. Your thoughts, feelings, words and actions impact what is attracted towards you and could be used to help you reach your Diamond Goal.

Your Thoughts, Energy and People

The thoughts you have send signals to others and it can also be used to attract certain situations and people towards you. I am not implying that you can use telepathy for all situations, but there's a certain influence your thoughts have towards situations. A lot of the time, we may be subconsciously attracting situations and particular people towards us. For example, have you ever had one of those moments when you had someone on your mind or even in the back of your mind and after a couple of days or even minutes, you see or receive a message from them? That may be the very law of attraction working! By being conscious of this, we can be aware of how our thoughts attract people and situations in order to help us reach our Diamond Goal.

Everything around us has been made from the unseen[8]. Our thoughts are unseen and have the power to bring our ideas into the seen world. For example, this book was once an unseen idea in my mind and is now a physical manifestation that is being held in your hand. Make a habit of guarding your mind because your thoughts are where most of your life's battles take

Our thoughts are unseen and have the power to bring our ideas into the seen world.

place[xiii]. We can find ourselves in any situation, but it is our mind-set that determines how we respond to those situations.

Our thoughts and state of mind will also attract the people we choose to surround ourselves with. We tend to draw the kind of people that are similar to ourselves. If we want to be inspired to reach our Diamond Goal, we need to surround ourselves with inspiring people. As we are the average of the five people we spend the most time with[xiv], it is important to intentionally be around people who are succeeding and reaching their goals. Are you choosing to surround yourself with people who inspire you? Challenge you? Stretch you? If we are not conscious and intentional about the people we surround ourselves with, we will be swept along without direction, thereby not realising the impact it's having on us and our future. Jim Rohn[xv] stated that any sane person would stop someone from immediately pushing them off a cliff, however, if the person nudged the person 'just a little' each day, they could gradually edge them off the cliff before they even realised! This shows the importance of how being aware of the people you surround yourself with is crucial to where you end up.

This reminds me of a time when I was working towards a Diamond Goal, and felt incredibly positive about it. However, there was one particular individual who just oozed negativity. I was so excited and positive that I didn't take note of their negative attitude. The person would make sly, condescending and discouraging comments. There were even times it got personal! They were like an energy leach – sucking all the positive energy in the room. When I met them initially, I could feel that their energy was in some way…'off' but could not quite put my finger on it. Intuitively, I knew something was not right. After repeatedly hearing their negative and narcissistic remarks, I decided to distance myself from them. The more I distanced myself, the more they decided to draw near to find an opportunity to interact with me. We were on different energy planes, and I felt a drop in my energy level each time they draw near. I took the decision to shorten interactions, distance myself and surround myself with people, coaches and mentors that were working on their own goals. This was one of my toughest experiences, but it taught me about the sensitivity of my thoughts, my energy and people.

Have you ever been around people that just like to moan and complain? Most of their speech is negative and you just find yourself feeling unhappy and uncomfortable around them! We all know of the saying 'misery loves company.' Well, people with a negative mindset operate at a low frequency and energy level. If you are in a positive state of mind, it is very unlikely that you will be around them for a very long period of time! The disparity between your energy levels will be significant and you will probably feel the urge to leave their presence. There may be times you feel tempted to have a moan or pity party, although appropriate at certain times and to the right people, it isn't going to get you closer to your goals! Surround yourself with successful people and create progressive steps of change. Where can you find these people? Some may be in your friendship circle, networking events or special occasions. The more you do this, the more likely you are to reach your goals.

Your Emotions and Your Words

Your emotions can be as powerful as your thoughts. Your thoughts create your feelings because how you feel is very much dependant on what you think. Some things might genuinely be upsetting, but in most cases, it is our programming and thought processes that dictates whether you are joyful or miserable about any given situation. It is your perspective that dictates how you feel. You can find yourself trapped in an unpleasant situation and though this is an

Your thoughts create your feelings because how you feel is very much dependant on what you think.

awful experience, it is still your thoughts that will cause your emotions to feel particular feelings. It is up to you to take responsibility and change your perspective of a situation even if you cannot change the situation itself. This can then have an impact on how you feel and what you say.

Your words have power. Words are like little containers holding manifestations of power within them. As you speak, they launch forward and roll out life events like a red carpet. There's a scripture that states "Death and Life are in the power of the tongue"8. This quote suggests that when you speak, you have the power to bring about life and fruitfulness, or death and decay. Use your words to bring about the result that you want to see, even if you do not see them yet.

Words can also influence how others think and feel towards you and can also help them decide on whether they want to know you or distance themselves from you. When we speak positive words and radiate energy to go forward, we inevitably feel empowered to take the right steps to reach our goals. Alternatively, when we speak negative words, we are influenced with a different sort of energy; an energy that can, and often does, lead to inaction. The unseen energy we wrap ourselves in can play a large part in the thoughts we have, the decisions we make, and the behaviours we exhibit.

> *When we speak positive words and radiate energy to go forward, we inevitably feel empowered to take the right steps to reach our goals.*

The words we speak to ourselves are even more important! The person you will be around all of your life is… You! So, your words will either empower or disempower you in reaching your goals. What words are you speaking to yourself and will these words empower you to reach your goals?

To show the importance of words, there was a study carried out by Dr Masaru Emoto[xvi]. He had different jars of water, and labelled the jars with either a positive word such as 'love' or a negative word such as 'hate.' He spoke over the jars with the labelled word, and then left them for some time. After a while, he used a microscope to look at the molecular structure of the water. Results from the study showed that the jars of water which had positive words and emotions spoken over them had a beautiful crystallised structure with each positive word for each jar reflecting a unique shape. However, the jars of water with negative words and emotions spoken over them had a disfigurement in structure. The water molecules were deformed and distorted. Applying this knowledge, we can see the power of our words and emotions. Our body is around 60% water[xvii], and so, if the words we speak have an influence on the molecular structure of water in a jar, you can imagine the impact on 60% of our body! This is why we need to be conscious of the words we speak and the emotions we feel as this has an impact on how our body responds.

Relating to your Diamond Goal, Napoleon Hill in his book 'Think and Grow Rich' emphasises that a person needs to feel a burning desire in order to reach their goals[xviii]. This burning desire is strongly linked to the emotion that pushes you into action. Feelings are vibrational energies that influence the way we use our words and ultimately, influence our actions. You can increase the 'burning desire' emotion by focusing on your *why*; the reason you set out your goal in the first place. In fact, imagining what would happen if you *didn't* reach your goal could

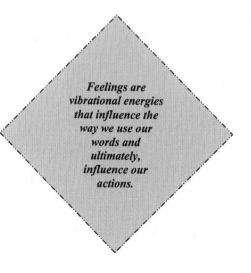

Feelings are vibrational energies that influence the way we use our words and ultimately, influence our actions.

be equally emotional. You could use this emotion to spur you into taking action. For example, if I didn't release this book, I would feel embarrassed and disappointed. My friends and family will be disappointed by my lack of dedication in completing my Diamond Goal. This encouraged me to be self-disciplined and dedicate time to its completion.

Your Actions

After all the internal processes, you then decide what action you are going to take to help you reach your Diamond Goal. Consequently, you have a choice of how you respond to particular situations. On your journey to success, you will experience disappointments. You can either choose to take responsibility or blame outside sources for unfavourable outcomes. If you choose to take responsibility, then you are ultimately empowered. Taking responsibility does not mean everything is your fault, it simply means that you have the power to change it. When facing challenges, you do not need to deal with it on your own, you can involve a mentor or someone more qualified to help you overcome that particular challenge. The important thing is that you are taking action.

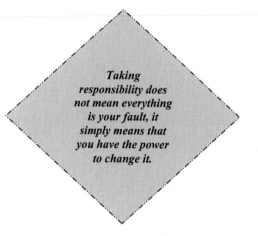

Taking responsibility does not mean everything is your fault, it simply means that you have the power to change it.

However, if you choose to blame the outside world such as your family, the government, the weather, you tend to disempower yourself from moving forward. Blaming everyone else for what is going wrong is incredibly unproductive to all, and does not help to build deeper relationships. Those relationships may be the very ones you need to move forward to achieve your life's purpose.

Sometimes, your reactions are subconscious and you may not even realise it. Defence mechanisms show up, thereby causing you to react abruptly rather than patiently responding. If you take a few seconds to become conscious of what is happening around you, it will help you to respond and act in an appropriate way. This can be easier said than done and takes a lot of practice before it becomes second nature, but the more we do it, the more effective it will be as a response to a difficult situation.

If a negative situation continues to occur frequently on the pursuit of your Diamond Goal, this may indicate that it is time to review and reflect on why it keeps reoccurring. Do you have a particular thought surrounding your goal? There may be an underlying belief or thought about a particular issue that continues to show. Alternatively, it could be life trying to teach you a lesson. Therefore, it's helpful to ask 'what lesson do I need to learn here?' Reflecting on this can give you an insight into the actions you need to take to effect a change in the situation.

In conclusion, your thoughts, emotions, words and actions all influence you on your journey to your Diamond Goal. They empower you to move from the stage of a rough diamond to a polished and more defined diamond. Use them in a positive manner to help you overcome challenges and focus on working towards your goals.

"Throughout human history, our greatest leaders and thinkers have used the power of words to transform our emotions, to enlist us in their causes, and to shape the course of destiny. Words can not only create emotions, they create actions. And from our actions flow the results of our lives."

Tony Robbinsxix

Key Points:

- Be aware of how your thoughts, energy and people influence you in reaching your goals.

- You have the power to use your emotions and words to help you take action.

- Choose to respond rather than react to challenging situations.

Reflections

What type of words have you used today - have they been more positive or negative?

_____

_____

_____

In what situations do you find yourself having negative thoughts?

_____

_____

_____

What emotion do you feel when you think about your goal?

_____

_____

_____

Who do you need to be around more that will be a good influence on your thinking?

_____

_____

_____

How can you practically fuel your burning desire?

_____

_____

_____

What action are you going to take today to get closer to your Diamond Goal?

_____

_____

_____

Success Step 4

The next time you feel negative about a situation; use powerful positive thoughts and words to respond.

◆ Chapter 5 ◆

◆ Chapter 5 ◆

Diamond Cutting:

Cutting Away Distractions

It is often quite difficult to identify the distractions that can lead us away from reaching our Diamond Goal. Distractions can come in the form of unfortunate circumstances, challenging obstacles or negative people. Sometimes, distractions happen over a long period of time, and sometimes they happen in a split second. During the diamond cutting process, the rough edges of the diamond are removed, and the remaining parts are refined and polished. We can liken the discarded 'rough' edges of the diamond to our daily distractions, they need to be removed in order for us to create a clear path towards our goal.

Circumstantial Winds

Circumstantial winds will blow and try to knock you off course; however, Jim Rohn states 'It is not the blowing of the wind but the setting of the sail'[13] that will determine your response. It is up to you to decide whether you will allow it to divert you, or whether you will set your sail towards the direction of your benefit. If you believe in God, then you have an additional helper to help you sail through. In fact, in my opinion, it is that very helper that will help you turn the situation around.

Some wind storms last longer than others, but with your eye set on the end goal and your strong *why* pushing you forward, you will be able to sail through. Remember that hard times are temporary and do not last. They are distractions that try to divert your attention to what is *really* important in helping you reach your goal.

People

We've looked at how the circumstantial winds can change, but what about people? Distractions can also come in the form of people's negative opinion of what you are doing.

It is important to remember that you are in control of how you respond to this. If you allow the negativity to affect you internally, it will disempower you. However, by focusing on your goal and reminding yourself of your why, you will be able to overcome the distraction.

The distraction could come in the form of rejection from others. Nobody likes or enjoys being rejected, but this may be a part of the process to successfully reach your Diamond Goals. One of the best ways to handle rejection is by attaching a productive and positive meaning to it. For example, if your application for your dream job was rejected, you may feel that you were not good enough for it. However, this could work in your favour. You could take the rejection as an opportunity to grow and learn something new, or see it as an open door to something even better.

I knew of a man in a company who had the lifestyle to dream of. He travelled the world, lived in a luxury home and positively impacted people everywhere he went. He always had a smile on his face and a joyful aura, and crowds would follow him just to be in his presence. Whilst he was delivering a training session, there was a phrase he used that has always stuck with me. He pointed to the projector and said "You see this jacuzzi, tub and lifestyle? All the smiles on people's faces? That is a result of all the rejections I faced!" In other words, it is because he had experienced so many rejections, it eventually led

him to the opportunity he truly sought. Each rejection you face in the journey towards your Diamond Goal will only inch you closer to its fulfilment.

When you have a particular goal or dream in mind, it is not surprising to find yourself against opposition. This can often come from those closest to you, which may genuinely shock you. When this happens, bear in mind that they may not be intentionally or even consciously trying to distract you. It can be for several reasons unbeknown to you.

People tend to feel uncomfortable when someone close to them is progressing at a rate faster than normal. They may then try to slow you down with their words and actions in an attempt to keep you at your current level. This makes them feel more comfortable and is a false illusion that they are preserving your relationship. This is particularly true if they are not progressing at the same rate as you. Remarks such as 'what's the point of doing that?' 'don't bother with that!' and 'you can't do it' are a few of the comments you may hear. This is just their defence mechanism. It is now your choice – do you let those words hold you down or do you overcome them and keep marching ahead? Choose to march ahead!

Sometimes, these experiences will be disheartening and distressing, but this is because of the 'crab mentality'xx. To understand the crab mentality, picture this: There are crabs in a bucket, all crammed in together. One crab sees a way out. So, the crab tries to climb out to escape, but as it does this, the other crabs reach out in an attempt to pull it back down. That sort of "If I can't get out… you can't either!" mindset is unhelpful and as a result, all crabs remain in the same place, and are trapped in the bucket! This what happens in life when one person is trying to reach further and achieve a goal. Even though their action may ultimately help those around them, others may not see it the same way and may often try to keep them down.

The best way to cut this distraction is to quietly remove yourself from the people that dampen your dream. This is hard to do especially if you are passionate. Sometimes, people do not see your vision until later on down the line.

People may also try to distract you by criticising your goal as a form of protection. In their own way (which may seem strange to you), they are trying to protect you from going in the wrong direction. It makes them feel anxious that you are going in a direction they do not agree with. Your burning desire and passion have launched you forward into new realms, and this is a huge paradigm shift for them. When surrounded by those who are not willing to take the journey with you or support you in any way, it will be best to disengage from such people and surround yourself with those who do.

When surrounded by those who are not willing to take the journey with or support you, it may be best to surround yourself with those who do.

Mastermind Group

You need to create or find your own mastermind group who will support you in your journey – I assure you, they exist! These people will encourage you, motivate you, stretch you and sharpen you to become even better. These people see and feel what you see and feel, and are part of your journey.

I remember when I was working towards my Diamond Goal of building a productive team; I had a group of four other women who were working towards the same goal. We connected on the phone each week, and kept each other accountable. It was a positive, yet challenging few months, but we were a powerful group of mastermind women forging ahead towards our goals. At the end of our dedication and consistent contact, we were able to create individual teams that were productive.

Mentors and Coaches

A way of cutting away distractions is by finding mentors and coaches that can help you reach your goal. If you are unable to physically meet mentors, finding a virtual one is also an option. By this, I mean you could find successful people who have been through your situation and have made it to the other side. This doesn't necessarily need to be someone you know; it could be a well-known author or motivational

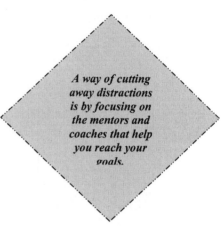

A way of cutting away distractions is by focusing on the mentors and coaches that help you reach your goals.

speaker. This may mean building your library of supportive materials, and constantly listening to them to sharpen your focus. To help you on your way, I have included some of my favourite books in the appendix.

There are many other ways in which people may try to stop you, but ultimately, it is up to you – will you listen to the distractions or decide to press on? Your mind-set and self-belief will be paramount to answering this. It is not strange to experience thoughts of doubt or fear. These are normal responses, but if you have a strong supportive network around you, they will help you move forward. Some mentors may be able to cheer you on, build your faith or divinely connect you with others that will help you on your journey. Tune in to them – they will play a major role in your diamond steps to success. However, it is important that you consider whom you take advice from. A question I was once asked when working on a Diamond Goal was "Would you ask an electrician or a plumber to fix your television?" If you want a fully functioning television, the obvious answer would be an electrician. Therefore, if you want advice from people, make sure you ask the relevant and appropriate person.

It is important that you consider whom you take advice from.

Although you can surely learn from others, asking advice from those who do not share your vision may not be the wisest idea. When people share advice, cautiously consider the advice they share and evaluate whether this will help you reach your goal.

If possible, it may be wise to find a coach who can help you progress by guiding you through the challenges you will face. Search for someone who has gone through what you are going through to help use their experience to motivate you. You need to be open to their direction and be humble to listen. Take heed and listen closely, the results in their life show that they know what they are talking about.

Accomplishments

One of the biggest forms of distraction comes from the destructive voice we hear from the inside of our minds. It is the self-doubt, the questioning and the voice of fear. You hear… 'Can I do it? Who am I to try? Others have failed, what makes me different?' As you allow these thoughts in, this can sap your energy, and you can find yourself spiralling down a rabbit hole.

There must be a way out! What I have found to be helpful in this situation is to take a detailed review of past accomplishments. Are there times you felt like you couldn't accomplish something, but then went ahead and did it? How did you feel when you accomplished it? Taking note of these elements of your journey and surrounding yourself with images of when you reached a previous goal can greatly help you increase in confidence and cut the distraction of self-doubt.

All in all, it is inevitable that you will experience distraction on your journey towards your Diamond Goals. It is not easy, but it is crucial to cut them out and focus on what you want to achieve. Drown self-doubt by surrounding yourself with people that motivate you and remember

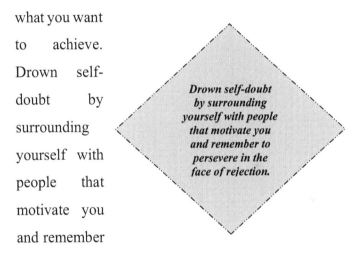

to persevere in the face of rejection.

"Starve your distraction, feed your focus"

Charmaine Haydenxxi

Key Points:

- You have the power to decide how you respond to circumstantial winds and challenging people.

- Cut away distractions by surrounding yourself with mentors and coaches.

- Use past achievements to boost your self-belief and confidence.

Reflections

What distractions commonly show up in your life when you are trying to reach your Diamond Goals?

_____

_____

_____

How do you respond to circumstantial winds?

_____

_____

_____

How will you respond to rejection and criticism?

_____

_____

_____

Who could be your mentor and/or coach?

_____

_____

_____

What have been your past achievements to date?

Success Step 6

Find one mentor who supports your goal, dream or desire and communicate with them at least once a week.

◆ Chapter 6 ◆

◆ Chapter 6 ◆

Sorting Diamonds:

Keeping Focus

During the process of reaching our goals, there is often a time (or several) that we feel like giving up. This especially happens when we come to the penultimate stage. Continuing with the diamond making analogy; once the diamonds have been cut, polished and shaped, it is now time for the producers to sort the diamonds into categories. This process takes extreme focus, precision and dedication. This can be likened to our journey towards our Diamond Goal. As you draw close to completion, it's often quite tempting to lose focus and give up

Marathon

Your journey to the successful completion of your goal is like a marathon – not a sprint. Just like the diamond process, your journey can be very long and sometimes arduous. If you think of a sprint, they are often very quick and short-lived. However, a marathon takes more time and you need to distribute your energy evenly over the length

Your journey to the successful completion of your goal is like a marathon – not a sprint.

of the run to reach the finish line. Therefore, on your journey, be patient with yourself and take breaks. Pace yourself and keep your focus on your goals.

I remember when I was running a marathon in the high altitudes of Utah to raise money for the True Health Foundation charity. I started off with a lot of energy, but when I got to the half way mark, I began to lose momentum. My Diamond Goal at the time was to complete the marathon. Therefore, to stay focused, I reminded myself of why I was running and paced myself steadily. As I ran, there were times it was necessary for me to take short breaks so I could regain my energy. When I saw my fellow runners, it gave me the motivation to keep going. During the last lap, my chest began to ache and my knees became weak. I slowed down my pace, took deep breaths and kept focus on my goal. In the end, I crossed the finish line and completed the run. My encouragement to you is take breaks when necessary, but keep focused on your goal!

Accountability

To keep focus, make yourself accountable to your goal. This could be through publicly declaring to others that you will finish a project or openly displaying your goal in a prominent place. Making yourself accountable to others applies the needed pressure to keep you focused. This is because if you find yourself derailing from your goal, others can help to remind you of what you set out to do. It may be nerve-racking, and may make you feel like avoiding the group of people, but it is an opportunity for you to stay on track.

Set Milestones

You can keep focused on your goal by setting milestones. Write the smaller steps of what you need to do in order to get to the next stage of your goal. By ticking these smaller milestones off as you go, you keep yourself motivated to keep going. This is especially useful when you have a long-term goal. You will know that you are making progress as you achieve each step and will ultimately reach your Diamond Goal.

For example, if you have a goal to attend a conference that costs £1,200, you can set smaller milestones of saving £100 per month at the beginning of the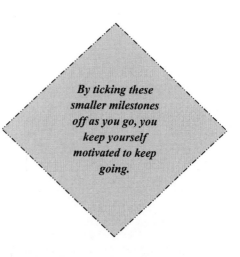

By ticking these smaller milestones off as you go, you keep yourself motivated to keep going.

year in order to purchase the ticket at the end of the year. Smaller milestones may include reserving a place on the guest list and sorting out travel. Small incremental steps no matter how small will edge you closer to reaching your Diamond Goal.

Write a Plan

When you have your Diamond Goal in mind, you would want to create a plan that accurately describes and outlines what it is you need to do so you can reach it successfully. This is similar to writing down your milestones, but involves more detail to how you want to achieve those milestones. This will keep you focused. The plan may be daily activities that lead to the weekly and monthly milestones.

For example, I remember when I was booked to do a speech in front of a large group of business builders in Bournemouth. I formulated a plan based on the concept of my speech, and then broke down the message across different slides. Each day, I wrote a checklist of what I would need in order to make the speech effective. These included the finding of images, personal anecdotes and the inspirational stories of others who had achieved their goals. I then would review and update this list daily. At the end of the week, I would catch up on any previously missed work that contributed to the end goal. When it came close to the end of the month, I would practice the speech repeatedly. Eventually, the day came when I was called to the stage to deliver my speech. I was able to speak in a clear concise way that delivered an impactful message to the audience. Because I had set out a plan and wrote it down, I was able to work accordingly and achieve my goal.

Keep Focused on what's Important

It is easy to lose momentum when your Diamond Goal is even more long term. This means that it takes more effort to keep focus. You will need to be dedicated and precise in how you use your time. When things are taking longer than we desire, we can sometimes just focus on the urgent tasks and ignore the important ones. We must distinguish between what is urgent and what is important. For example, if you were given a project at work to complete and you just found out your

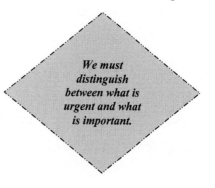

We must distinguish between what is urgent and what is important.

television broke down; though this is an urgent matter, your work project ought to be your utmost priority at that moment, and it may be the main source of income that will help pay to fix your television. Many urgent matters will try to divert your focus, but keep track on what is more important.

Our Habits

Our habits also have a part to play in whether we reach our goals or not. If we haven't developed the habit of consistency and discipline, it will be hard for us to keep focus. Our brains are accustomed to thinking in a particular way, and this can be difficult to change especially when working towards our Diamond Goal[xxii]. However, through the repetition of practising positive habits and affirmations, we can put our mind in the right state to achieve success.

Learning from the Unexpected

Sometimes it's easy to lose focus when things are not going the way we planned. Even though we have set out a plan and repeated positive habits, the unexpected can still happen. We may feel burnt out or experience a loss of motivation. Instead of reacting negatively, you can reflect on what the situation has caused you to learn. Did you feel burnt out because you had to take a break to rest your mind and rejuvenate? Did the

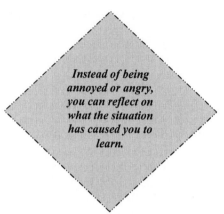

Instead of being annoyed or angry, you can reflect on what the situation has caused you to learn.

loss in motivation happen because you needed to remind yourself of your *why*? These could all be the learnings you could take from when things don't go as planned.

Things may not go to plan because of our own mistakes. Sometimes we need to be vigilant so that we do not create our own obstacles when trying to reach our goal. For example, leaving a data file for a business presentation at home by mistake. The best thing to do would have been to put it in your bag when you finished preparing the night before. But sometimes, mistakes do happen, we are human after all and as such, no one is perfect! The most important thing to remember is not to beat yourself up about it when they do happen. We need to make sure we do not allow those feelings of guilt to derail our focus and demotivate us. Learn from the situation quickly, rectify the problem and keep focused.

When you feel like Giving Up

When you are almost at the finishing line, you may feel like giving up on your goal. Keep going! When people say 'Never Give Up' it is usually because they know that it is so much easier to! But ask yourself, what will giving up cost you? Will it cost you the time you had already dedicated to making it happen? Will it cost you your self-confidence when you know that if you pushed through, you would have made it? Giving up is an easier option and many opt for it because they lack the will to keep trying. Regardless of how many people give up

Regardless of how many people give up around you, decide to press on and to never give up.

around you, decide to press on. It may not be perfect, but you would have greater respect for yourself because you had completed something that you set out to do.

In conclusion, the journey to your Diamond Goal takes focus. It is very important to balance your energy for the duration of your goal and take breaks *when necessary*. To focus on your goal, make yourself accountable, set millstones and a daily plan. Distinguish what is important and work on your habits, knowing that mistakes are inevitable. Your goal is causing you to grow, and you will surely reach it if you never give up!

"Success is not final, Failure is not fatal. It is the courage to continue that counts."

Winston Churchillxxiii

<u>Key Points:</u>

- At the penultimate stage of reaching your goal, remember to always keep focused.

- Make yourself accountable, set milestones and create a plan for your Diamond Goal.

- Never give up on what you can achieve and what you have seen people succeed at.

Reflections

What can you do to balance your energy whilst working on your Diamond Goal?

_____

_____

_____

How can you make yourself accountable regarding your goals?

_____

_____

_____

What milestones can you set to reach your goals?

_____

_____

_____

What is your plan to reaching your goals?

_____

_____

_____

What habits can you build to help reach your goals?

_____

_____

_____

When you feel like giving up, what can you do to keep going?

Success Step 6

Write the milestones you need to reach to achieve your Diamond Goal.

Chapter 7

◆ Chapter 7 ◆

Jewellery Setting:

Bringing it all Together

The final stage of the diamond process is jewellery setting. This is the result of the diamond process from the beginning to the sorting of diamonds. When it comes to reaching your Diamond Goal, it is time to position yourself and decide on where you want your goal to make the most impact. In comparison, when the diamond is ready, the diamond setter affixes the precious stone into the piece of jewellery that is best suited to the quality of the diamond. This may be on a ring, a neckless or even a watch. Upon completion, the diamond is used to enhance the quality of the jewellery. This is similar to reaching your Diamond Goal. All the work and effort you have put into making your goal a reality has now made you more valuable not only to yourself, but to others.

Consolidating the Process

Now that you are closer to reaching your Diamond Goal, it is time to pull all the steps you have learned together. An example of when I did this was when I had the goal of winning an impromptu public speaking contest. The contest was hosted by an organisation called Toastmastersxxiv, a non-profit educational organisation.

These are the steps I used:

Step 1: Seeing the End from the Beginning

Before I even entered the competition, I visualised what it would be like to win a public speaking contest. I knew it would be something that would make me more valuable as it would enhance my communication skills. When the opportunity came forth to enter an impromptu speaking competition, I decided to make it a Diamond Goal. I used my five senses to help enhance my thoughts about how it would feel to go through the competition and win.

Step 2: Identifying What My Diamond Goal was Worth

I knew that entering this competition would be worth it because it would provide me with the courage to help others in their development of their own public speaking journey. For example, coaching young people on how to communicate and speak confidently was an aspect that made this goal worth it. Therefore, I dedicated time to prepare for the competition despite the cost and sacrifice it would take. I attended weekly meetings at Toastmasters and signed up as a participant for the competition. There were occasions when I felt tired and demotivated, but I had good people around me that encouraged me to keep going. The commitment took faith, but because of the conviction I felt, I persevered.

Step 3: Removing Limiting Beliefs and Fear

There were times I had limiting beliefs about whether *I* could really win a public speaking competition, especially as I had only been a member of Toastmasters for a short period of time. However, I worked on removing those limiting beliefs and fear with more empowering truth-filled affirmations such as 'I can do this'.

Step 4 - Using my Thoughts, Emotions, Words and Actions

I used positive thoughts such as 'I am an authentic speaker,' positive emotions of joy, words of affirmation such as 'I can win this competition' and actions such as publicly practicing impromptu speeches in order to help me reach my goal. I also had to deal with certain challenges that meant I could not practice as much as I would have liked to. However, instead of negatively reacting to the challenges, I decided to practice with a friend via short voice notes between lunch breaks.

Step 5 - Cutting Away Distractions

During the journey towards my goal, there were many distractions. These included noise, interruptions, clutter, hunger, doubt – you name it! To deal with this, I ensured I was in touch with mentors and coaches who had previously dealt with similar issues whilst preparing for a speaking engagement. They were able to provide me with tips on ways to deal with the distractions and shared some successful techniques for the day of the competition. They also reminded me of my past achievements, and this kept me motivated.

Step 6: Keeping Focus

Once the day of the competition drew close, I set myself the milestone of answering impromptu questions daily and putting into practice tips from my mentor. I made a plan of what I would wear for the competition, how I would get there and what techniques I could use to answer the impromptu question given. I made myself accountable to others and was delighted to see them show up on the day as support. During the times I felt like giving up, I was encouraged not to. When the day of the competition arrived, I was as prepared as I thought I could be and it paid off. All the steps tied in together, and I was announced as the winner of the impromptu speech competition.

My encouragement to you is to use these steps in consolidation to successfully reach your Diamond Goal.

Using Your Words to Add Value

When you have achieved your Diamond Goal, you can use your words to continue to add value to yourself and others. In the front of the book, you will see the letters I, A, M, S, U, C, C, E, S and S highlighted. They spell out 'I Am Success.' This is because if you believe this, you will inevitably become a success and add value to the lives of others. Using your words can help you share the learnings you've gained from achieving your goal with others so you can be a source of inspiration for them to achieve their own. When they hear you making confessions such as 'I Am Success', you then have the power to

Using your words can help you share the learnings you've gained from achieving your goal with others to inspire them to achieve their own.

confidently inspire and influence them by adding value to their lives.

Positioning Yourself

Positioning yourself in places where you can add value to others means being visible in order for others to benefit from your goal. Depending on what your goal is, you may want to position yourself in a space where you can market your goal if it is a product or service. This may be at an event where you know that people who need your service or product will be. It also includes advertising your product or service on social media platforms such as Facebook, Instagram, LinkedIn etc.

An example of this was shown when I was growing publicity about a product I was selling. I made it a habit to post valuable content on social media at least three times a week – if not every day. This included advertising the benefits of the products, posting stories about my personal journey in business and writing inspirational messages. This resulted in people not only knowing about the product, but also gave them the opportunity to know about me as an individual. Thus, they were not only able to benefit from the product, but they also benefitted from my experiences.

Reward Yourself and Celebrate

When you achieve your Diamond Goal, celebrate! This is also a form of adding value to yourself. As you have dedicated time working on your goal, ensure that you reward yourself. This boosts your self-esteem and teaches your inner child that hard work pays off which will in turn encourage you to accomplish more

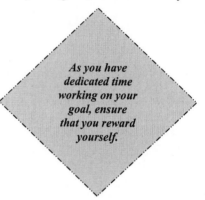

As you have dedicated time working on your goal, ensure that you reward yourself.

Diamond Goals. As you do this, you continue to add value and strengthen to your character. As you continue to grow and achieve your goals, you will inevitably inspire others too.

In conclusion, remember that reaching your Diamond Goals is a process and like the diamond, it needs to go through specific steps. It is important to consolidate all the steps to achieve the desired outcome. Remember to position yourself in the right spaces that will add value to others, whilst using your words and experiences to inspire them in their own journey.

Last but not least, celebrate the successful completion of your goals and use this to motivate yourself to achieve even greater endeavours.

With that being said, I wish you all the best in reaching your Diamond Goals through your Diamond Steps To Success!

"SUCCESS is when I add value to MYSELF.

SIGNIFICANCE is when I add value to OTHERS."

John C. Maxwellxxv

Key Points:

- Use the six steps from previous chapters to achieve your Diamond Goal.

- Position yourself to showcase your goals in order to add value to others.

- Celebrate the achievement of your goals.

Reflections

How can you bring all the steps together to achieve your Diamond Goal?

_____

_____

_____

Seeing the End from the Beginning:

_____

_____

_____

Identifying What your Diamond Goal is Worth:

_____

_____

_____

Removing Limiting Beliefs and Fear:

_____

_____

_____

Using your Thoughts, Emotions, Words and Actions:

_____

_____

_____

Cutting Away Distractions:

_____

_____

Keeping Focused:

_____

_____

_____

Success Step 7

Write down one way reaching your Diamond Goal will add value to yourself and others.

Remember to always confess:

I AM SUCCESS!

◆ End Quotes ◆

End Quotes

"Keep the image of the end from the beginning and you will inevitably take the necessary steps to make it your reality!"

Joyce Oyedele

"Nothing in the world is worth having or worth doing unless it means effort, pain, difficulty... I have never in my life envied a human being who led an easy life. I have envied a great many people who led difficult lives and led them well."

Theodore Roosevelt

"You are far too smart to be the only thing standing in your way."

Emma Kate

"Throughout human history, our greatest leaders and thinkers have used the power of words to transform our emotions, to enlist us in their causes, and to shape the course of destiny. Words can not only create emotions, they create actions. And from our actions flow the results of our lives."

Tony Robbins

"Starve your distraction… Feed your focus"

Charmaine Hayden

"Success is not final, Failure is not fatal. It is the courage to continue that counts."

Winston Churchill

"SUCCESS is when I add value to MYSELF. SIGNIFICANCE is when I add value to OTHERS."

John C. Maxwell

◆ Appendix ◆

Appendix
My 25 Top Rated Books

1. The Bible
2. Success Principals – Jack Canfield
3. The Dynamic Laws of Prosperity – Catherine Ponder
4. The Compound Effect – Darren Hardy
5. 7 Habits of Highly Successful People – Stephen Covey
6. Three Feet From Gold – Lechter and Reid
7. Purpose Driven Life – Rick Warren
8. The 10X Rule – Grant Cardone
9. Think and Grow Rich: A Black Choice – Dennis Kimbro
10. Think and Grow Rich – Napoleon Hill

11. The Power of Positive Thinking – Norman Vincent Peale

12. Battlefield of the Mind – Joyce Meyer

13. Secrets of the Millionaire Mind – T. Harv Eker

14. The Business School for People who like Helping People – Robert Kiyosaki

15. Laws of Growth – John Maxwell

16. Failing Forward – John Maxwell

17. Thinking for a Change – John Maxwell

18. Business Secrets from the Bible – Daniel Lapin

19. The Magic of Thinking Big – David Schwartz

20. How to Win friends and Influence People in the Digital Age – Dale Carnegie and Associates

21. You Were Born Rich – Bob Proctor

22. The Psychology of Winning – Dr Denis Waitley

23. Building Your Network Marketing Business – Jim Rohn

24. Challenge to Succeed – Jim Rohn

25. The New Psycho-Cybernetics: A Mind Technology for Living Your Life Without Limits Audiobook – Original recording - Maxwell Maltz and Dan Kennedy

◆ Endnotes ◆

Endnotes

i Maltz, M. and Powers, M. (2010) *Psycho-cybernetics*. Chatsworth, Calif.: Wilshire Book Co.

ii Maltz, M. and Powers, M. (2010) *Psycho-cybernetics*. Chatsworth, Calif.: Wilshire Book Co.

iii Meyer, J. (2018). The Everyday Life Bible. New York: Hachette Nashville.

iv Munroe, M. (2003). *Understanding the purpose and power of prayer*. New Kensington, PA: Whitaker House.

v YouTube. (2019). *When things go wrong, don't go with them*. [online] Available at: https://www.youtube.com/watch?v=dpJVloQHpRM [Accessed 12 Feb. 2019].

vi Goodreads.com. (2019). *A quote by Theodore Roosevelt*. [online] Available at: https://www.goodreads.com/quotes/312751-nothing-in-the-world-is-worth-having-or-worth-doing [Accessed 6 Feb. 2019].

vii Wells, D. and Slusher, H. (1983). *Schaum's outline of theory and problems of physics for engineering and science*. New York: McGraw-Hill.

viii Jeffers, S. (2011). *Feel the fear and do it anyway*. New York: Simon & Schuster Audio.

ix Biblegateway.com. (2019). *BibleGateway.com: A searchable online Bible in over 150 versions and 50 languages.*. [online] Available at: https://www.biblegateway.com/ [Accessed 6 Feb. 2019].

x Networkmarketingpro.com. (2016). *Network Marketing Coaching.* [online] Available at: https://networkmarketingpro.com/coaching/ [Accessed 6 Feb. 2019].

xi Goodreads.com. (2019). *Erin Hanson Quotes (Author of Reverie).* [online]

xii Daeyna Jackson: Inspiring Confidence. (2019). *5 Effective Ways To Overcome Limiting Beliefs As Female Entrepreneurs | Daeyna Jackson: Inspiring Confidence.* [online] Available at: https://daeyna.com/5-effective-ways-to-overcome-limiting-beliefs-as-female-entrepreneurs/ [Accessed 6 Feb. 2019].

xiii Meyer, J. (2008) *Battlefield of the mind.* London: Hodder & Stoughton.

xiv Maxwell, J. (1998). *The 21 irrefutable laws of leadership.* Nashville, Tenn.: Thomas Nelson.

xv *Challenge to Succeed.* (2001). [Audiobook] Directed by J. Rohn. Jim Rohn International (2001).

xvi Emoto, M. (2005). *The hidden messages in water.* New York: ATRIA Books.

xvii ThoughtCo. (2019). *How Much of the Human Body Is Water?.* [online] Available at: https://www.thoughtco.com/how-much-of-your-body-is-water-609406 [Accessed 6 Feb. 2019].

xviii HILL, N. (1987). *Think and grow rich.* New York, Fawcett Books.

xix A-Z Quotes. (2019). *Tony Robbins Quote*. [online] Available at: https://www.azquotes.com/quote/1062154 [Accessed 15 May 2019].

xx Peng, L. (2016). *Good Intentions Are Not Enough: Why We Fail at Helping Others*. Singapore: World Scientific Publishing Co. Ptc. Ltd, p.104.

xxi Hayden, C. (2019). *Starve your distractions feed your focus*. [online] Charmaine hayden. Available at: https://charmainehayden.wordpress.com/2015/01/14/starve-your-distractions-feed-your-focus/ [Accessed 7 Feb. 2019].

xxii Loder, V. (2019) *How To Rewire Your Brain For Happiness*, *Forbes.com*. Available at: https://www.forbes.com/sites/vanessaloder/2015/03/18/how-to-rewire-your-brain-for-happiness/#30447e2759ef (Accessed: 13 February 2019).

xxiii BrainyQuote. (2019). *Winston Churchill Quotes*. [online] Available at: https://www.brainyquote.com/quotes/winston_churchill_124653 [Accessed 6 Feb. 2019].

xxiv Toastmasters.org. (2019). *Toastmasters International -Home*. [online] Available at: https://www.toastmasters.org/ [Accessed 11 Feb. 2019].

xxv A-Z Quotes. (2019). *John C. Maxwell Quote*. [online] Available at: https://www.azquotes.com/quote/859588 [Accessed 27 May 2019].

Endnotes

Printed by Amazon Italia Logistica S.r.l.
Torrazza Piemonte (TO), Italy